LIFE.TIMES SIX

Intimate glimpses into the joys and struggles
of six generations of Northland immigrants

To Those Who Value Humanity

BY MARGARET OLSON WEBSTER

Copyright © 2007 Text and Paintings by Margaret Webster

All rights reserved. No part of this book may be reproduced or transmitted in any form, except short excerpts for review or educational purposes, without written permission of the publisher.

Published by Bluepearl Books
10008 422 Street
Tamarack, MN 55785

Printed and bound in the United States of America
by Bang Printing
Brainerd, Minnesota

ISBN: 0-9722378-3-6

Acknowledgements

Grateful acknowledgement is made to the many people who willingly took part in candid interviews and who provided the basis for this book.

Technical help and advice were expertly and freely given by the following people: JoAnne Collins (McGregor Printing), Paul Webster, Kaija Webster, Perry Webster, Andrew Webster, Rick Johnson (Rick's Printing), Lawrence Berg (photography), Phil Wagner (Bang Printing), Sharon Filliatrault, Karin McGinnis, Jinx Engstrom and Delores Walli.

I especially want to thank my husband, Dan, for his help and encouragement on a daily basis.

CONTENTS

Forward
Entry
Do You Dance?
Colorful Years
What's It Worth To You?
Why Marry, Lady?

Chapter 1: Farewells	1
Mourning My Motherland	2
I Grew to Love it Like My Motherland	4
In My Trunk	5
Dear momma	6
Tell Tale Discovery	7
War - The Cruelty of It	8
House or Home?	9
Beearies - Berry Pie Recipe	10
Bear in the Beearries	11
Pie on Lace	12
My Berry Pie	13
Impi	14
Chapter 2: In My Day	16
In My Day, The Second Generation	17
Place	19
An Ever Present Help	20
Mojakka Recipe	21
Mojakka Spice	22
Last Flash	24
Have We Learned Anything Yet?	25
Norwegian Potato Dumplings	26
We 'Klubbed' the Pastor	27
War - Is It Noble?	28
Chapter 3: The Work of It	29
We Can Do It All	30
Ella May Was a Cat Skinner	31
Lutefisk and Lefse - Recipe	32
Useless War?	34
Nurse, I'm So Glad You're Here	35
All Things Come to Him (or Her) Who Waits	36
The Birthday Party	37
Walking is My Heritage	38

Chapter 4: Free to Be 39
    Free to Be 40
    Faith by Osmosis 42
    Pizza and Crepes 43
    In a Word: Absurd 44
    Cabbage Recipe 45
    There's a Cat Buried Under That Tree 46

Chapter 5: Been There, Done That 48
    Been There, Done That 49
    Fast Food Beware! 50
    Life Cycle 51
    Sweet Sweet Maple 52
    Swedish Pancake recipe 53
    Concert in the Swamp 54
    Swamp Quadrant 55
    War of Opportunity 56
    Selling Oneself as a Woman 57

Chapter 6: A Hundred Years of Change 58
    Time Pushes Me 59
    Party Line 60
    Technically Speaking 62
    Back from Iraq? 63
    Purrfect Morn 64
    May 13th 64
    Smoothy 65
    Eternal Circle 66

FORWARD

As we remember the past and relate to the present our thoughts center on human experience. How do generations survive? What joys, sorrows, concerns, rewards are experienced? Assumptions are sometimes made that poetry is fiction. This book is a result of many interviews, deep observations gathered over a lifetime of acute awareness of reality around me. My mother died nearly thirty years ago, my sister is no longer mentally able to relate. I looked around me at our small old school/club house and realized that women working there to prepare for a community dinner are my mothers, sisters and grandmothers. Each has a rich tapestry of experience. This book records a tiny sample of those lives.

A variety of voices speak, even within one chapter.

Many cultures, including ours, to a point, look at life as cyclic in nature. These reoccurring experiences may include working with, thus observing nature's great and small cycles; fashion in most aspects; beliefs; economics, and human life itself. Folk sayings reflect this attitude:
- "What goes around comes around."
- "Everything old is new again."
- "The more things change the more they stay the same"
- "Eternity is being 'born again'"
- "The only thing constant is change"
- "This has happened before".
- " What has been will be again." Ecclesiastics 2: 7

Poems and illustrations in this book intend to reflect circles and cycles. Some are poignant, humorous, reflective of life from the generation turning twenty in 1900 to those reaching that "age of maturity" in 2000. Chapters are given in increments of twenty years.

I sincerely hope these collected words will bring you both joy and thoughtfulness. Thank you for responding so well to my other books ;A FUNNY THING HAPPENED ON THE WAY TO THE CEMETERY and ARE ALL THE HEROES GONE?
I do not label this as a "woman's book", as men's exploits have been told for many years without being labeled "men's books."

Margaret Olson Webster

DEFINING ISSUES OF EVERY GENERATION

Very basic to life would be one's entry into it: Birth. Woman's unique attribute as mothers has been both blessing and curse. When asked about life's greatest joy most women responded without hesitation: "Having children". That joy has a cost in economic repression, loss of autonomy, health factors, and other life choices,(including control of the number of children a woman "delivers", a very important factor in the very survival of our world). Limited resources will not suffice for the snowballing overpopulation. Until women are respected enough to be free of forced roles as sex object and producer of children the world is in peril.

The birth process today is more centered on the mother than when our time cycle began. Midwifery, a choice dictated to many women in our area in first and second generations has now been a choice for two out of three of my daughter-in- laws. The other was able to have a cesarean section to deliver an eleven pound baby.

ENTRY

CHAPTER 1
Born 1880

I came into the world in a most beautiful spot…
Suomi ,Finland, Mammi
In a holy sauna, though not fired too hot.

CHAPTER 2
Born 1900

Difficult birth, ninth child: opened my eyes
New land, sauna floor.
Mother would never hear my birthing cries.

CHAPTER 3
Born 1920

I first opened my eyes: saw a wild world, fair:
Log house, plank door
Katio* came to farm, from middle of nowhere!

CHAPTER 4
Born 1940

A shanty "maternity home" in tiny town
Railroad, church and store
And a woman doctor of widespread renown.

CHAPTER 5
Born 1960

A midwife brought me into this world of progress
Anomaly to the core
Back to ancient instincts, technology less.

CHAPTER 6
Born 1980

Hospital, convenient for doctor, sterile, effective
Bigger town: semi-four
Less personal, mom and babe "doing well."

*healer/midwife

WHY MARRY-LADY?

Human relationships, here represented by the institution of marriage, are certainly influenced by customs, expectations and pressures surrounding social groups of people throughout time.

I married for physical safety:
Roaming armies in my home land
Unspeakable acts, silent scream
Destruction, rape, murder by the band   Twenty in 1900
Protection vanished as a dream
Mourn my husband as a victim.

When I married it was a quest:
Sail the seas to a golden place,
My young man and I sure it was best   Twenty in 1920
Hardship and work resolutely faced,
Adventure turned to cold stone wall
In the face of a villain: alcohol.

"Shameful" the woman living single:
Not much credit or voiced respect
For a "lonely woman", pockets a-jingle.
"No suitors, not even a good prospect?   Twenty in 1940
Respectable, but lonely as I grew older
As in age, our bond only grew colder.

Man and woman were created for sex:
Answering those strong innate urges.
As if desired pleasure fell under a hex   Twenty in 1960
Time, in its ever measured way, purges.
Pain, not answering a pleasant need,
Former fertility dampened the deed.

Man provides magnificent income:
Huge house, cars, travel, beautiful toys
Crash, bust, we lost all and then some.   Twenty in 1980
Poverty provided no accustomed joys
So my mate decided to break his vow
And I, a struggling single mother now.

I have a "relationship", no legal knot
I've seen pain, disappointment, entrapment.
Marriage for safety, or because "he was hot".   Twenty in 2000
Common goals, money don't make the gent.
Nor society know what is best,
Guess time will be my true test

DO YOU DANCE?

Dance? Where has the music gone?   1st GENERATION
Drowned out from dusk to dawn,
Can't hear a single chord or beat.
Make hay, grow food…working feet
No time, energy. Can't think I should.
Where is the instrument if I could?

Walk or ski a dozen miles   2nd GENERATION
Just to see the happy smiles
On faces as they whirl in time
Singing words come out in rhyme
Schottische, waltz or polka late,
Chances good you'll find your mate.

Bigger halls in which to dance   3rd GENERATION
Makeup, swirling skirts enhance
Movement to a big band sound.
Feet don't seem to touch the ground
Meet many people of all places
Bubbling, swirling, different races.

"Be bop a Lulu, that's my Baby"   4th GENERATION
Sock hops, rock and roll and maybe
A little twist or Limbo thrown in.
Pony tails, bobby socks and bobby pin.
Dancing fast and dancing hard: a must.
But be the dancer someone can trust.

I see the dance floor as much like life-   5th GENERATION
Won't dance backward to be a good wife.
Not lockstep, do my own thing-
Love living= have a good fling
Yes, band sometimes plays out of tune,
We Like that better than romantic croon.

Great, great, great grandma, the bam,   6th GENERATION
Bam, ba bam and occasional wham
Might seem to disturb your very soul
Loud sounds would take their toll.
You wouldn't find peace in the word.
Sorry to hear what you have heard.

Dance? Where has the music gone?

DO YOU DANCE?

Dancing and the music facilitate well basic human expression of life, attitudes, emotions. Even the popularity of various musical instruments is very reflective and cyclic. Often called a "melting pot", the United States reflects character of various countries through dance. In our area it was Nordic polka, schottische and waltz. Currently you might see Spain, Africa, or modern U.S. reflected on the dance floor (or on several popular "dance shows".)

COLORFUL YEARS

"Champaign- What a wonderful color for a sink"
" In the old days beige was ecru I think."
" It's tan, man.."

Color's more than simple "red", named for fruit
veggies, sky, water, rocks…all to suit
what sells well.

Long ago we fought the redcoats: blue and gray,
to Europe in Khaki, then navy had it's say.
Sports carry Peri.   (Periwinkle blue)

Dishes, potato peelers, ice picks, clothing-green.
First manufactured in mass, economy seen.
No doubt "out".

Lots of rooms, outfits were in Dramatic maroon.
Variety of items were marooned with gray.
In movie: groovy

The fifties brought cars and clothes "hot" pink.
Grey, now "charcoal" is what we think
cool at school.

In sixties mom's kitchen was Seafoam Green.
Touches of bright-Navaho Red then seen
no doubt "out".

Big business now chooses colors two by two
names trends: "in" fads for you and you
The New Hue?

Green becomes a forest, Maroon turns to wine
Consumers accept their plan, call it fine.
Buy the dye.

Black and white, no color at all, very sheik.
Worn casual, or "black tie", not bleak
Gone:neon.

Back to black?

COLORFUL YEARS
In our technical and economically pushed world, even something as basic as our use of color is manipulated and controlled by a few financially successful people and corporations. Nature, however, will always be our base for reoccurring colorful appreciation and inspiration.

WHAT'S IT WORTH TO YOU?

"I need 14 eggs, not just a dozen,"　　　Early 1900's
store manager says eggs too small.
Where, now, will I get money for
Underwear for Sulo and Nels?
Jacob's working at the lumber camp,
But payday is not soon enough for us.
Sister Sophie in Duluth wonders
Why she never hears from me…
Where are three pennies for a postcard?

I got the teaching job today!　　　1920s and 30s
The school board says I will not earn
As much as a man as I'm inferior
"You know you need to find a man
to support you. We pay more to men:
they need to support a wife and family.
You are lucky to have this job,
Remember, if you marry or worse yet
Become 'with child' it's over for you."

I set aside my salary for an entire year　　　1960s
To buy the property for our home:
Husband says " I bought this land for her".
I gardened, refinished furniture, canned
And managed our budget to build the house.
I pounded nails, put up insulation, painted.
Husband says "I built this house for her".
Women are not meant to have an ego,
Still can't think of equality with man.

High court ruled today, landmark case.　　　Early 2000s
A woman finally proved she got less pay
Than men employed to do the same work.
"Too late" the court pontificated.
Too late for equality, security or self worth
It will be an example throughout the land
Women certainly will never be worth
As much as is a man. Equality laws:
When will they come true?

Chapter 1

FAREWELLS

**BORN IN 1880
IMMIGRATED TO UNITED STATES IN 1900**

*I came into the world in a most beautiful spot...
Suomi, Finland, Mammi
In a holy sauna, though not fired too hot.*

MOURNING MY MOTHERLAND

"Let's leave this oppression and hunger!" he announced,
"to new world of freedom and plenty": Finland renounced.
'Accept his decisions, I've taken a vow-but go now?'
'He is my husband and head, to his word I bow,'
Starvation bread from tree bark fresh in my mind,
Cruel and inhuman treatment could stay behind.

Oh how I rued the decision, on the vast open sea.
The sail upset new life now dependent within me,
as waves lashed our ship, violently tossed.
Trip to the "New World" came with a cost.
No respite, shelter, comfort appeared-misery in crowd.
'Is this a sign of things to come?'... Never ask out loud.

Oh, we arrived at our homestead by train line
And a trail marked by tree slashes, bear sign.
Isolation, broken only by a neighbor, out of curiosity
Came to see who fellow wilderness strugglers could be.
Thank God he spoke Finnish; musical and expressive,
Not new language; chopped, limited, almost repressive.

We built the Sauna first: cleansing, holy, sheltering.
Soon we were protected, refreshed and sweltering.
There I birthed my first baby; alone, yet at peace.
I nursed from nature, infant from me. Wonders never cease.
Of twelve children delivered ten would survive,
Such unending work to keep them alive.

Oh I miss my Motherland-a sadness never ceasing,
Yet blessings here are numerous and pleasing.
I miss the sparkling, shining lakes, the sky so blue.
I miss the trees: Koivu, Pihlaja and Haapoja too.
Birch, Mountain Ash and Poplar where we roam
Aren't the old friendly trees 'round us at home.

I miss the smell of Finland's earth and air
Of ancient kacloons*, baking bread so fair.
I still hang my loaves on the ceiling!
To use old ways gives me some healing.
I love the new old forest and the northern lights,
But do so long for home during long dark nights.

I came from Duluth by train, rowed across a lake, then walked to the homestead. I was guided by slashes on the trees along the way. It was evening, but I got there before dark.

I GREW TO LOVE IT LIKE MY MOTHERLAND

I cried when first I saw it
Not tears of frustration or loss,
Or regret of our decision to roam.
But because our homestead was so like
beloved countryside at home.

I am speaking purely of the land,
Heavily forested, with so many lakes.
Instant water for people, cattle and soul,
Trips to sauna, fishing boat or moonlit shore,
Leave a person peaceful and whole.

Rocks of every size and hue
Reminiscent of home, Finland built on stone.
We pick them from future fields we need to till,
 fences, saunas, foundations, roadbeds
or into swamps for solid fill.

So many trees I've seen before:
Sacred birch, pine, and larch, poplar and ash.
We busily cut, just to clear field or garden spot
Build homes, barns, fences or hay sheds,
Some left on ground to rot.

Coyotes wail a plaintive song,
Wolves join voices in the howl of wildlife.
Some are silent: bear, turtles, rabbits and deer.
Our children have interesting pets, skunks are what
one might call them here.

So the land supplies what we need
To survive in this wild and lonely country.
Go to the store, on path, with never a road defiled.
We trade things we have grown, harvested, trapped
Learn to use gifts of the wild.

IN MY TRUNK

"Wear as much of your clothing as will fit,
allow room for other things within this trunk".
Necessities of life will add up, bit by bit
No room for nostalgia or useless junk.

" I will share my spices", Mother calmly said,
as she packed cinnamon, cardamom, allspice.
"And some clothing for your new hand hewn bed,
Two large sheets and comforter should suffice."

"You will need a starter for your fiilie bunk"
Soak a small rag in my thick sour cream,
Hope you will have fresh milk in which to dunk,
Food to remind you of home, your dream."

I will pack my needlework, useful items all,
Tablecloths, baby baptismal dress, knit hose'…
Even a cheery sampler to hang on the wall.
One beautiful handkerchief for my nose.

Two plates, two cups, forks and spoons, and a jar.
(fill that with salt and seal it tight}Soap-one bar…
Paper, envelopes, pen, ink-write in my own hand
To let them know how things are in that new land.

DEAR MOMMA

Dear Momma,
   My labor only lasted half a day,
Grandbaby named Pearl
   Your travail much on my mind,
Your eight deliveries.

   You learned the value of human life,
Birthed precious babies
   To care for, see life's joys and trials.
There for lifetimes.

   For four this was never to be:
soon dead, gone.
   As if they had not been at all.
Pain, only yours.

   Then we other three, your babie
Grown to adult
   Chose to die to you, your realm
New World called.

   So you have only one child there,
Help for age
   To see those grandchildren born
Hold in reality.

   So I hold you in my mind and love
Momma, now grand.
   I wish I could be transported there,
homeland and you.

This letter will not be sent, only a happy birth announcement. No guilt, loneliness or pain will be revealed. A sea of lost human contact will separate the sender from her mother.

TELL TALE DISCOVERY

I wish I hadn't seen it-
Family after family
Destroyed by demon rum.

Few women strong enough
Time after time
to deny father dear his fun.

Worries, fears, insecurities
Pain after pain
Can and must be made numb

Is your mate a "mean drunk?"
Cruelty after cruelty
Angry, mean and dumb?

Or is he soppy, sappy sweet,
Betrayal after betrayal
Squander the farm-then some?

Here's Father, home from town.
Sniff after sniff…
Smell indiscretion: Confront the bum

'YOU'VE BEEN EATING ICE CREAM !'

WAR- THE CRUELTY OF IT

Occupation of oppression:
   Torture, murder, starvation, rape and subjugation
Meant to kill a nation, person by person
    Those countries never killed our spirit-sisu.

Lottery of death:
    Brothers, sons, husbands in their prime
Tearful farewells, men marched to a city far away
     Some fated for a lifetime in the occupier's army.

Immigration, Hope:
    Peace, hard work, deprivation, struggle,
But at least we don't eat tree bark bread
    No one knocks on our door with ill intent.

Fleeting Peace:
    Then the new country enters war*.
"I'm not raising "cannon fodder"
     Men grown to feed a conflagration

War is Hell .

*World War 1

HOUSE OR HOME?

I knew it was a bachelor's house
A poor man who had no spouse:
To embroider, crochet or even tat.
To decorate, fancy this or that;
A doily for one upholstered chair
 Fancy cloth to cover dresser bare,
 Beautiful crocheted edged curtain.
 I sense, almost know for certain,
 View with some dismay
 That he likes it that way.

BEAR IN THE BEEARRIES

Two molasses tins and a shotgun pail*
Held high, as I wade through the swale.
Now I can smell the berries I so desire,
See plants that also live in the brier.

But what's that other odor so offensive
It puts picker on immediate defensive?
Yes, old Otso the bear has discovered too,
There's berries here, more than a few.

Do I leave this patch at a hurried pace,
To look for another picking place?
Or do I hum loudly and off key,
And hope Otso also respects me?

*A tall, narrow aluminum pail,
which carries well through
the brambles holds a
good amount.

BEEARRIE

The sweet, precious sound of the word
Rolls off the tongue in a special way...
One of few words spoken with such relish
Sweet drops of flavor, treasured gift of nature..
Collected to eat with cream at the table
Or made into jelly or jam with fresh bread,
Cooked into quart jars for the winter,
Or served in a tasty crisp piecrust but never,
I repeat...never let someone see you eat one
In the berry patch, whether blueberry, strawberry,
Pincherry, chokecherry or wintergreen.
A picker so imprudent must learn to wait until
Word is given after all pails are heaping..
Then feast on the tree, bush, or vine...
 Part of the sacred ceremony of berry picking.

•Many smells help you identify a good place to find berries, it could be the odor of the plants themselves, or the plants which usually grow in nearby area. You do not want to smell the unpleasant, uniquely glandular smell of the bear. If you do, you must decide weather to leave or to co-exist. At all costs you want to make sure that you do not get between a mother and her cub(s).

•The location of a good berry patch is often a well-guarded secret as the fruit was a good source of winter vitamins, as well as pleasure.

PIE ON LACE

We have settled in this far place
Sparsely settled, out of touch
with most of the human race.

Forests, swamps, lakes fill our space
Shelter, Warmth: so very much,
plus food to feed our face.

Fish, meat and nuts are at home base
to amply fill our storage hutch.
But what's my favorite grace?

Strawberries, Raspberries, and in case
they aren't available as such,
berry pie on table covered in
lace.

MY BERRY PIE

CRUST:
- 1 cup lard
- 3 cups finely milled flour
- salt
- pinch of baking powder if you have it

Cut together using two knives or wire pastry cutter if you have one. Lard should be the size of a pea when you are done. Mix in a little cold water until you can roll it out. Be careful not to add too much or stir too much or it will be sticky. Flour table or board and roll out (ball about the size of 3 eggs.) with rolling pin or straight bottle. Fold in half and lift into pie tin or flat soup dish.

FILLING:
Clean leaves and bugs from berries, enough to fill your crust. Put sugar to taste and a little flour to thicken, a little butter if you like.

Roll out top crust and place it, pinching the edges of the crust to seal shut. Slit to let steam out.

BAKE about 1 hour in medium hot oven. If it starts to get too brown put paper over it.

IMPI   THEY SAY

I hear the devil, stomping in…
Shiny black features   "Not fit to hear…
Eyes glowing red, hate   Nick's obscenities cut,
I married him   contaminate the air.
                                Neighbor scared me"

A new baby kicking to life within
Fears devil already   "They had many babies
Children starve and freeze he wanted farm help
I am despised   Little food or clothing,
                                life was hard."

Nick thinks I don't know, no idea
Searing, tearing poker   "Post partem depression?
Will bring more babies   Use birth control? Not
More abuse   even if it existed.
                                Life cheap."

Tears into me viciously carelessly
Baby just tore out of me   "She was very young
Pain is life-life is pain   when brought from Finland-
Voices taunt   what joy did she have?
                                no love."

Can't meet precious baby's needs
Cries drive me insane   "He wouldn't even buy
Is it my fault?   her a spool of thread.
Evil woman   No wonder she's crazy
                                blame her?"

Baby is freezing…turning blue
Warm in oven?   "She really lost it…
Last blanket a rag.   Put baby in oven.
Lost God   Really bad news,
                                lost faith"

Devil takes my baby…gone
Away forever   " Will you take this baby
In white shroud   for, awhile?'
Why live?   In dishtowel freezing.
                                Might live?"

Will I see him again? Hold him?
Love my children   "Want your baby now?
Wish voices would stop.   'Keep him' Nick said,
Precious gone   'Got enough help.'
                                  So we did."

Devil drags me fighting to his car
Going where, where?   "He put her far away
Forced away from hell…   Needn't remember her.
Caged beast.   so forget her cries…
                                  Better gone."

Voices still echo echo in my head
Cold shadows of people   "Mental Institution;
Real? Or more devils?   not good in those days.
Why me?   Real hell I hear…
                                  Why her?"

God has given me new words
Fools devil's helpers   "She spoke a jibberish mishmash
No familiar face   No one understands…
Floating time.   no one visited.
                                  Years and years."

My mother comes now, smiling
I see her clearly   "Died in that institution…
Fly me safe home.   saw apparitions.
God loves me?   Died away there…
                                  a blessing."

If truth be known only the intensity of Impi's situation separates it from the plight of many women everywhere, even today, but especially in first generation immigrants, here in the United States.

Chapter 2

IN MY DAY

BORN IN 1900
SECOND GENERATION

Difficult birth, ninth child: opened my eyes
New land, sauna floor.
Mother would never hear my birthing cries.

IN MY DAY: THE SECOND GENERATION

In my day…
A girl was lucky to get to school
I wore the school shoes* every second day-
Sister Hannah schooled them on others.
Halftime's "all we needed to be good mothers".

In my day…
In the eyes of our city teacher
Neither we country boys or girls knew much.
We were almost impossible to teach…
Must have been our "foreign speech".

In my day…
Walking to school might be fun or a challenge
Depending on sun, wind, snow or sleet.
Sometimes, we skated on smooth lake ice,
Making the trip to school quite nice.

In my day…
Socializing between genders was on the sly,
You were better off not raising your eye
When some young man tried to pass you a note
Or the whole class might see what he wrote.

In my day…
You must memorize to understand the subject:
Arithmetic, geography or spelling
Penmanship, reading, poetry, or facts from the past:
Learn "by heart" or your grade lowered fast.

In my day…
Never said "I don't like that" when offered food,
As it was usually better than eating nothing.
I worry today that we're so refined and wealthy
We lost most sense about eating healthy.

*two sisters share one pair of shoes fit to wear to school

In my day…
"Fun" was a basket social, making valentines,
Dances on occasion, and even swimming parties.
Games like "tag", "hide and seek", "anti I over" were fine
But even in games we walked a fine line.

In my day…
No travel to places far away, no fuss made over us-
Just do what you must, and be glad you're alive.
No shooting, killing or maiming was considered "fun"
No chatting for hours…there was work to be done.

In my day…
You learned many skills: sewing and sowing*,
Canning and gardening, milking and mowing*,
picking rocks and berries, cleaning and child care,
fire starting and even, on occasion, cutting hair.

In my day…
We were raised to be wives and mothers
In that order. Walk the line, work hard,
Take God seriously, keep His commands,
And take as religiously your husband's demands.

* planting crops
* cutting hay or putting it into the hay mow.

PLACE

Grand buildings, roads and vistas
I hear about in our "geography" class
I wouldn't trade for swimming in pure water,
Or skating on ice, frozen as if dark glass,
Or for what I see as I climb a tree…

My father says it will come to no good
To dig that huge ditch with a great machine.
"We need our lakes and blueberry patches,
Roads take land, especially one I've seen
Covering land with sheets of cement."

Buildings tightly fit together with wood,
The scent and shape of trees still very real.
Or the pungent smell of the root cellar:
Potatoes, rutabagas, carrots for a winter meal.
Secure, ready for storms: Abundant life.

I'm surprised at nearly ninety when
People ask "How did you manage to survive
With so little? Didn't you want to roam?"
Now I wonder at the surprising array of products,
Food, clothing, entertainment and home,
Superficial, confusing and shallow.

AN EVER PRESENT HELP

There is a spirit surrounding me,
Yet not suppressing me
as life is prone to do.
The depth I can not fathom,
It accepts my limitations,
Loves me each day anew.

I know God well enough to ask
Any type of favor
Or seek comfort in any grief.
Trust, faith and obedience
will give me comfort, peace,
and trust in eternal relief.

I don't always understand
Omnipotence or presence
or how to pray aright
But please help me make the
Fall Mojakka taste good,
and serve enough bread tonight.

MOJAKKA RECIPE

1 lb beef/venison/ or pork
6 medium potatoes
rutabaga to taste
onion/celery to taste
6 medium carrots
Bay leaf
1 t. salt - to taste
allspice
pepper

Cube the meat (1/2 ") and brown in heavy skillet. Place in soup kettle,(may rinse skillet) and add water to cover all, simmer. Peel, cube the potatoes (1/2 ") and cook with meat.
Mince remaining vegetables fairly fine and add to kettle.
Add spices whole or ground: (if spices are whole, use porous bag)
Bring to boil quickly, simmer for at least one hour.

- leftover meat may be used instead.
- Porous bag may be cheese cloth and store string.

Mojakka is a staff of life type of food, a stew made with venison, beef and or pork meat: potatoes, carrots and rutabagas onions, sometimes celery cooked together with a porous bag of spices.

MOJAKKA SPICE
Women's Zest Can't Be Contained by Pure White Wrapping

Wrapped in white, tied with a sash:
     baptism, confirmation, marriage and burial,
hidden zest inside.

Spotless white cloth, tied in a tight covering
   Contains, covers, disguises
Hot, darkly exotic spices.

Sharply dried Bay leaf spikes through the cloth
   Seeks freedom from confinement
Unique, dangerous, pleasant.

Allspice, many intriguing flavors yet untasted
   Rolled tightly into a tiny ball
Zesty, influential, exploding.

Use in limited quantity, berries of fire
   Pepper wakes up the tongue
Sometimes burning the taster.

Innocent, decent and pure, the spices wait
   Tiny, innocuous, smiling
To enhance the soup of life.

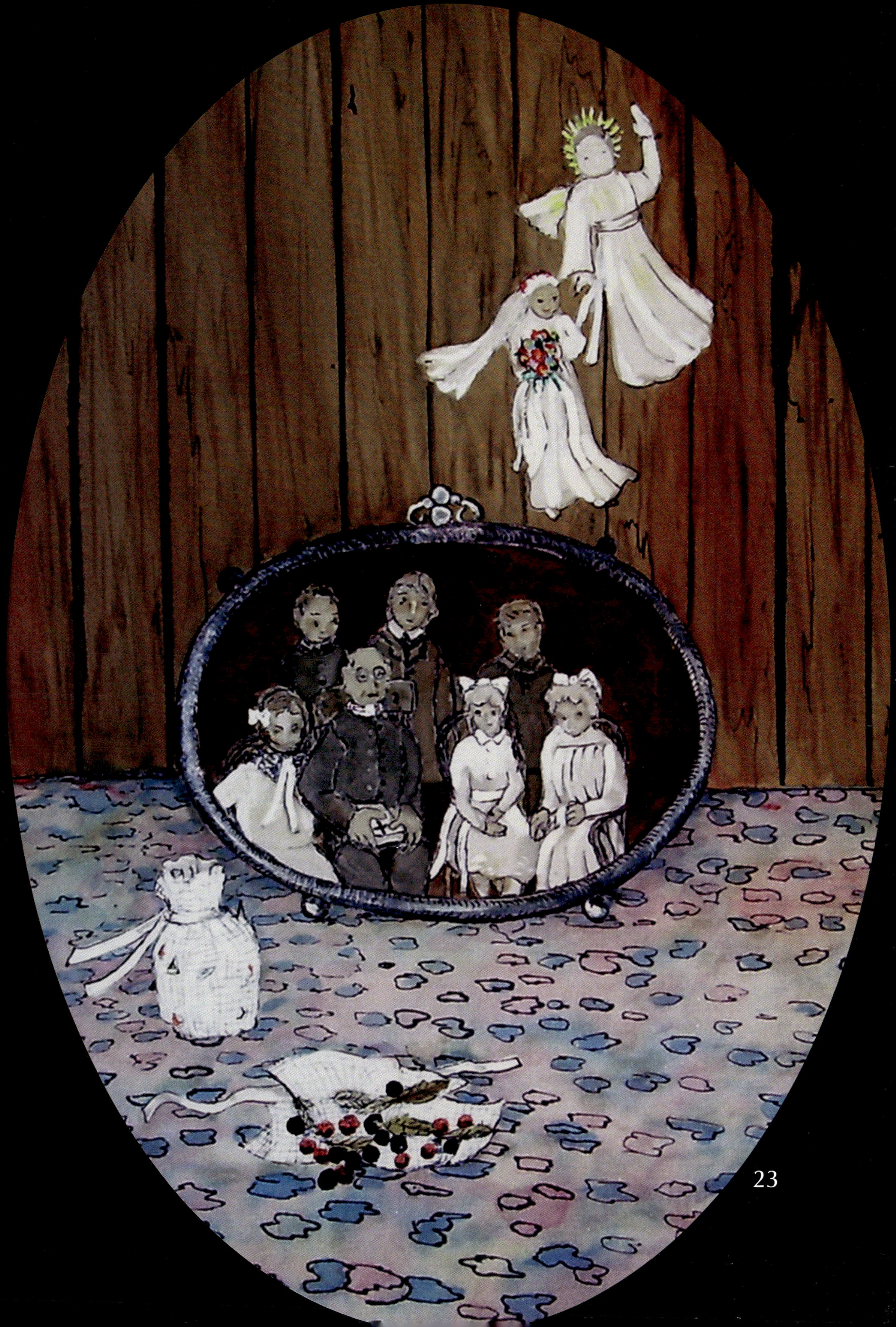

LAST FLASH

Hi Dauno!
He turned and nodded
With a smile that came from his eyes.

In line
To share the soup of life
Carefully cooked by Lakeside's* women.

Dark windows
Revealed overpowering flash
Blue, iridescent encompassing camera

Gave mood
Of eternal power
To this simple Lakeside dinner.

Dauno finished
Walked out the door
Rain pelted his face with force.

He turned
Back to the clubroom
But he was no longer there

His eyes
No longer smiled,
His soul was no longer in them.

The women
Saw then: they knew
The face of death, so near.

His body
Fought a good fight
For weeks he tried to live.

Last photo
Of life had been taken
His camera out of life's film.

*early schoolhouse/community club

HAVE WE LEARNED ANYTHING YET?

My parents left homeland for many reasons.
One of them, unforgiving, unbending attitude
Involved with faith in higher power.

Now, having lived here for countless seasons
I see the very same rigid, self righteous demeanor,
Giving "backsliders" an angry glower.

" They play cards, work on holy days of rest,
dance wildly, dress that way too. Read bad books.
Things have gone unforgivingly sour"

"They read the same Bible, why can't they see
their interpretation is so wrong? Bound for hell.
Where in pain they must cower."

" Our kids won't play with theirs, if we have our say.
We speak only when telling them of error, but
Friendship can never really flower."

"If we had our way we'd punish them more severely,
change their evil minds for good, now we can only
give them our scary looks so dour."

I can only listen to angry differences expressed,
Think within my soul, that with peaceful meditation
Earth could be a golden bower.

NORWEGIAN POTATO DUMPLINGS

Preheat water in a heavy (I like cast iron) deep pan filled to 4 or 5 inches. Simmer. Dumplings will be placed in boiling water to cover.

GRIND into rectangle cake pan   1 large sweet onion
                                8 LARGE brown potatoes

(Grind the onions in one end of the pan for mixing with the meatballs. Grind the potatoes into the other end of the pan for making the dough. Be sure to save the potato's juice.)

MIX & MAKE INTO MEATBALLS: 1 lb ground pork
                            1 large, ground sweet onion
                            1 t. salt
                            Pepper to taste

MIX & MAKE POTATO FLOUR: ground potatoes and juice, flour and salt (to taste) until it forms a loose dough.

In your well-floured hand, make a flat patty of the potato dough, as thin as you can. Wrap the dough around the meatball and seal shut with your fingers. Slip the dough-covered meatball into the simmering water.

SIMMER: for at least 1 hour
LIFT GENTLY: with a slotted spoon every 15 minutes to avoid sticking to bottom of pan.

SERVE WITH BROTH TO TASTE.
Apple sauce is good with them.
Leftovers may be fried or warmed in broth.

* Work quickly with potatoes, as they darken quickly.
* Keep potatoes dry, do not soak in water.

WE " KLUBBED" THE PASTOR

Have you had the pleasure to eat
an incredible Norwegian treat?
You know, then, flavor can't be beat.

"Klub" doesn't have a good ring
so we call them potato dumpling
and of their merits we lustily sing.

Our pastor's last name was Aase
So I figured that likely he'd be
Pleased to eat a Klub, so we'd see.

"Haven't had klub in a decade"
he said as at the table he stayed,
soon all gone, all that I had made.

One klub is all I usually et,
Couldn't eat three on a bet.
Now then, I remember it yet!

He was built kinda slight
but held more than he might,
Young guy put four klub out of sight

Ya. Downed four weighty balls.
"Pastor sure ate lots", pa recalls,
Then left to make pastorial calls."

A miracle of Norwegian scope
this Norski began to pray and hope
That pastor Aase didn't explode.

WAR-IS IT NOBLE?

Save the world:
   Sail off across the sea to fight
For justice, freedom, (maybe greed?)
   Two brothers left our backwoods farm

Patriotism high:
   Even for very young like me
Songs of battle, rage and victory
   Sung around the community piano

Work harder:
   Milk cows, harvest forest
Grow those crops and herds
   Make up for missing men.

Caskets arrive
   Black bordered envelopes delivered
Men are just as dead
   Whether killed here or "over there"
Hell worldwide

Chapter 3

THE WORK OF IT

BORN IN 1920
20 YEARS OLD IN 1940

I first opened my eyes: saw a wild world fair
Log house, plank door
Katio* came to farm, in this remote place!

* healer, midwife

WE CAN DO IT ALL

What is my life about, you ask.
I've been almost to busy to think about that.
Guess I think about life as a task.
Not simple, because I must wear many a hat

I have given birth to six babies
Learned they don't call it labor for naught
Many husbands left home or farm
Aren't here to help as I think they ought

Some women I know took "jobs"
While husband was at war or away
We didn't make money in gobs
Man's pride kept good pay at bay

"No woman should make as much as a man"
" My wife doesn't have to work-
just works at the factory because she can"
"She'll run the house too, never shirk"

I find joy in many things I can do…
making a house a home, raising children,
cooking, cleaning and reading too.
 pulled many a calf, butchered many a hen.
.

If I could have a dream come true
It would be that woman be on equal base,
Whatever in life she decides to do
Equality would be the consistent case.

ELLA MAY WAS A CAT SKINNER

Five foot two
Steely blue eyes
She could take care of herself

Wiry, strong
One hundred pounds
She could take care of life

Determined
Set in her jaw
She could take care of mate

Had one life
Mother of four
She could take care of kids

Raised them up
Then shocked us all
She could take care of gossip

Moved away
Took on an earth mover
She could take care of man's work

Moved the earth
Ravaged brush and rocks
She could take care of caterpillar

Heavy work
Not done by a women
She could take care of breaking ground

* Cat skinner: an operator of heavy, tracked earth moving equipment.

LEFSE

One huge potato (6-7inch) will make 10 medium sized lefse.

Peel, dice, SALT and cook POTATO or potatoes in just enough water to prevent burning or sticking. When the potato is tender remove from heat, mash well. Add 2 T. heavy CREAM and 3 T BUTTER.

Cool at least to body temperature. Add FLOUR until you have a very soft dough. The softer you can leave dough the better your lefse will be.

Fix a canvas or tight cloth on your bread board, generously flour. Turn out about two cups of dough, give it a couple of kneads. Cut it into pieces size of large egg.

Roll out very thin.

Fold in half to place easily on your range top (today: on the lefse grill.) Fire should be medium hot. Open out lefse quickly. Adjust location on range so that the lefse don't burn, but cook quickly.

When lefse shows bubbles turn it quickly with a long slender flat stick.

Cool on rack.

We are apt to top it with butter only. (Swedes use sugar!)

We usually make at least 70 lefse or 7 recipes.

LUTEFISK AND LEFSE

I married a Norwegian,
Much to my family's chagrin.
Learning some Norski ways
Took many challenging days.

The smell of Lutefisk cooking
For ten years sent me looking
For healing, settling 'fresh air'
"morning sickness" is not fair.

After a decade I learned the trick:
Eat lutefisk to get lefse, not sick
I go to great lengths to make the treat
Potatoes were never so good to eat.

The thing that I don't understand:
That Norwegians don't demand
To eat this potato treasure daily
Not just on Christmas so gaily.

USELESS WAR?

Violence technical
  "The war to end all wars"…just a misnomer?
A second "World War", Korea, Vietnam
   Drafted and volunteer trained to fight.

Women fill labor void
  "Rosie the riveter"* not just a label
for women in war plants and farm,
    as always, working for men gone to war.

Respected, self sufficient
  Shoved aside as men marched home…
Forced back to second class
   After tasting sweet independence?

Dual role born of need
  Work out, care for home and family
Double the responsibility, expectations and work
   Born of war, now seen often.

War at home

*A nickname for women working in aviation and war plants.

NURSE, I'M SO GLAD YOU'RE HERE

Nurse…
I'm so glad you're here
Now,
Cool hand upon my
Brow
Took a bullet in my
Face
But you are here, soothing
Grace.
Legs are gone-war is
Hell
But you are here, I'll get
Well
Nurse…
I'm so glad you're here

Nurse…
I'm so glad you're here
Caring
Focused, seeing how I'm
Faring
I know now…this solder's
Dying
Help me die, I know you're
Trying.
Nurse,
I'm so glad you're here.

Nurse…
I'm so glad you're here
Tears
Still you calm my
Fear
Dressed in white, cross of
Red
Stay near me now, near my
Bed
MOTHER
I'm so glad you're here

ALL THINGS COME TO HIM (OR HER) WHO WAITS

Ken waits for the world hunger meeting to solve some problems,
Ina waits to serve and clean up after supper for those who got home late.
Ken hopes to publicize a program to rid the world of hate
Ina waits for that teen to come home safely from that first date.
And they both want and work for the world to be a better place.

Ina waits for an end to the labor of bringing another child into the world,
Ken is off to see that farm labor gets fair pay.
Ina sees the kids at play, after working so very hard all day.
Ken has been at a Farmer's Union meeting all day today:
And they both want and work for the world to be a better place.

Ken works to promote sustainable ag,
Ina waits for the hay to dry, and begins to pray
That the kids will be safe as she rakes the hay.
Ken speaks for the cause on T.V., plans what to say.
And they both want and work for the world to be a better place.

Ina returns from work in home health care.
"Oh no, how'd those darn cows break out?"
"Kids, let's go-this is what farming is all about".
Ken's meeting has accomplished much, without doubt.
And they both want and work for the world to be a better place.

With their toddlers, tweens, teens and beyond
Ina is organizing, conferring and caring.
With groups, committees and the media pairing,
Ken is organizing, conferring and caring.
And they both want and work for the world to be a better place.

All that difficult, intense and caring work by Ina brings
A family of wonderful people with honor in their eyes.
Somehow, her selfless service buys
Opportunity for Ken to accomplish his highs,
And they both want and work for the world to be a better place.

THE BIRTHDAY PARTY

"Ahti-fold his knees up…
Jacob-under his arms-lift more
I'll throw the last of the shoes
From out of the closet floor."
Hide father from our guests.

"Sleep peacefully in your Piilo Paikka"*
sleep the sleep of your alcohol swoon-
You consumed it like it was water…
Hush!…neighbors will be here soon."
You better be very quiet.

"Anderson's are coming up the drive"
"Has anyone cut the birthday cake?"
"Hurry, shut the closet door…
Now let's hope Pa doesn't wake."
"Hello, so glad that you have come."

"Where's the old boy with the birthday?"
"The head of our household is on a quest…
But now let's all enjoy cake and coffeeia"
"Yah, just be sure to wish father the best".
Too bad we missed him, good by."

"When he wakes will he show regret
for boozing our entire life away…
or will he be very angry with me
that he celebrated too soon in the day?
We will have our pride preserved."

* piilo paikka: hide away

WALKING IS MY HERITAGE

Walking is my heritage
My route…one that has been well walked before me,
This unpaved narrow country lane has borne the weight
Of many moods and modes of errands.

The sweet pungent smoke
Which has curled up from the Walli sauna
Through dusk for nearly a hundred years
Puts me in touch with my world, now and then.

Yeasty, the smell of the earth
Is good as it rises after the rain, rich and real,
Birch, aspen, pine, maple and oak. Tamarack, sumac
Swampgrass, cattail, and wild rose grow as if forever.

The Hunnuri Ghost House
Home of the local Kaatilo,
Who handled births and medical needs
As she saw fit, flamboyant,
Not caring how others evalued behavior.

Proud old white schoolhouse
Scene of a new language struggle, books and chalk,
Funerals, parties, war projects, dances and talks: Whose
Large long windows turn to gold in the setting sun.

Mother, were windows gold
As you sprightly hiked to dance or spelling bee?
Or hurried home with pails of berries, or turned the corner
In the flivver of your new suitor?

Uncle Ted in his pickup…
Saw more on this road than I hope to. Numbered the trees
Knew when one rabbit visited another. Never before so still
In granite garden. The end of his walk and mine.

The wide gold band on my finger
Links me with his mother. She traveled this road,
My grandmother, offering life and love and service,
Sharing her skills and her songs.

Now I walk this road for my life:
What will it mean to others that I've moved this gravel,
If ever so slightly in my daily journey"
Walking is my heritage.

Chapter 4

FREE TO BE

**BORN IN 1940
TWENTY YEARS OLD IN 1960**

*A shanty "maternity home" in tiny town
Railroad, church and store
And a woman doctor of widespread renown*

FREE TO BE

She is free to be
(If she raises her hand),
An answer person: move class along.
She could even be a little smart…
As long as a male plays superior part.

She is free to be
(if she is very exceptional)
A student of higher learning,
To become a nurse or a teacher,
not doctor, lawyer, architect, or preacher.

Joyce was free to be
A mother, a family woman.
She left academics in grade ten
To nurture children and mate,
not free now to flirt or date.

Helen was free to be
A person who studied
Piano, and played at "doings".
One of two females earning
A chance for higher learning.

Karen was free to be
Embarrassed , teased,
Hassled and hustled.
Males couldn't let the fact rest
She was quite bigger in her breast

Carolyn was free to be
Dreaming unbeknown
Of being a race car driver.
Wild, crazy, never to be true
As cancer hit at only forty two.

Bonnie was free to be
Quiet and non-committal
Who knows what was behind
Those sparkly blue eyes?
No one knew, least of all guys.

Margaret is free to be
A person who "does art".
No study of it, but lots of practice…
" Go down to grade three and four,
 paint a nice design on their door."

Deanna is free to be
A person who hunts and fishes
A super athlete, who plays basketball-
If you are guarding this player so fine
You're too delicate to cross time line*.

Most are free to be,
If she practices some decorum
(Doesn't wear skirts too short},
Shoppers, dancers or Roller skaters,
Fans of male sports and even daters.

* A basketball rule for girls which prohibited use of more than half the gym floor.

FAITH BY OSMOSIS

It's there, just like the air we breathe…
Not something we talk over much,,,
Unless somebody dies.

Certainly, no question about it we go
Through Sunday School, confirmation.
Became religiously wise?

Learn creeds, commands, and verses.
But to nity-gritty life decisions
Find few real true ties.

Learn from whispers 'round the corners
Sex is worse than murder, hate or greed,
Even telling lies.

But one wise older teacher told me true,
That if we love and honor God, then we
To skies will rise.

PIZZA AND CREPES

It's kind of a crazy world out there
I was 18 years before I would dare
leave my home for "big" cities glare.
No university in my childhood lair.

Sheltered life, never out of the state;
left for the "U" to pursue my fate.
Have to tell you: I was quite afraid
Wondered if I could make the grade.

Learned many a new way and fact
To make up for the polish I lacked
I chose to study Home Ec. and art
Things learned did gave me a start

I learned that Italians had a food
called Pizza, surprisingly good
possessing a flavor really nice,
once you get used to all the spice.

Swedish pancakes are really crepes
Curtains are sometimes called drapes
Brand new oven design is microwave
Many new rules on how "ladies" behave
.
Art fits in categories one can label
A wild story in English is termed fable.
You must identify an artist by his work
And memorize every little painting quirk

I learned that a gal from "Podum Junction
Could learn some new ways to function
In lots of ways beyond just knowledge
This girl is glad she got to college.

IN A WORD: ABSURD

You're telling me
that the seed I see,
no bigger than then a dot
can and will grow to be

bigger than my head?
Only needs a rich bed
of soil in garden lot,
well watered and well fed?

All this cabbage seed
is going to need
it has already got,
but freedom from a weed.

If it must always vie:
Too many plants close by,
Competition way too hot
It will surely die.

Plants will just not thrive,
they'll not stay alive,
will be over wrought,
maturity will not arrive.

Can't humans see what's true?
Growing plants give a clue
to truth we've fought:
we've bred too big a crew.

If we keep the current rate,
Unconcerned when we mate,
we'll deserve what we've got:
war, hunger, global warming, hate.

In a word: absurd.

QUICK CABBAGE

Slice cabbage, first halving it then placing flat side
down and cutting fine. (allow at least 1 cup per person)

Brown 2 T. fine bread crumbs for each cup of cabbage in
1 T butter. (These may be made from dried bread, crumbed
in blender or rolled in plastic bag)

Put just enough water in cooking kettle to make steam,
cook cabbage for four minutes,
then drain if necessary,
top with crumbs

THERE'S A CAT BURIED UNDER THAT TREE

Nobody knows but me…
There's a cat buried under that tree.
A cat whose huge golden eyes
No longer look up at the skies
A tiger named Johan Sebastian Bach,
'J .S. Bach' scratched on a flat rock.

Small…when the cat's heart ceased to beat
The tree now stands a mighty eighty feet
And the special family member beneath
Has likely disappeared into the heath.
Not even the marker is there to see,
Nobody knows he's existed but me.

Nobody knows but me…
And I wonder where they could be,
Marbles: blue swirled, yellow, red and green
Are underground, where they can't be seen
Left there on a beautiful long ago spring day
When marbles was a game to play.

Then over there, under the sod in back
Remains of the house, (or tarpaper shack).
So cold…snow drifted unmelted to quilt
It, too, was a fine house when built
Bulldozed away when new house came to be
And nobody knows where but me.

This might be an answer to why
I study the farm as I drive by
At the place I lived for a third of my life
live nearby, as a mother and wife.
Sorrow, joy, humor, regrets came to be.
And nobody knows but me.

THERE'S A CAT BURIED UNDER THAT TREE

A haze of lavender memory
Crowds out bright reality

Chapter 5

BEEN THERE-
DONE THAT

BORN IN 1960
20 YEARS OLD IN 1980

A midwife brought me into this world of progress
Anomaly to the core
Back to ancient instincts, technology less.

BEEN THERE, DONE THAT

Society, after eons of suppression,
Just realizing the mistake of oppression.
Allowing females to fulfill their potential,
An enlightenment which should benefit all.
Been there…done that!

Many careers are now available to us,
To be a carpenter no longer ignites a fuss.
I could be a scientist or an astronaut,
Or teach at the "U" without second thought.
Been there, done that.

Climb any mountain I want to master,
Do any math problem, and do it faster
Decide to have children or stay single
Travel the wide world over, mingle.
Been there, done that.

Still…a glass ceiling, men have an edge
You are considered pushy if you wedge
Too far into "male only" domain
So you tolerate the gender bane
Been there, done that.

FAST FOOD BEWARE!

Here's a Norman Rockwell* for you…
Sitting at a table set with silver, plates, food, beverage-
Talking face to face?

It's rather upsetting to me, too.
I had no choice of menu, no fried foods so fine-
Milk-where's my soda?

I don't know exactly what to do…
With silver silver, glass glass, china china and all-
Not Christmas dinner?

Eat a salad, eat an entrée, and soup on cue?
"burgers and fries" are what I wrap around
fast food for me.

Let me call someone on my cell-whew-
Can't eat, converse face to face, too real..
I Say "My bad?"

* Norman Rockwell-mid twentieth century painter/idealized traditional America

SPIRITUAL CYCLE

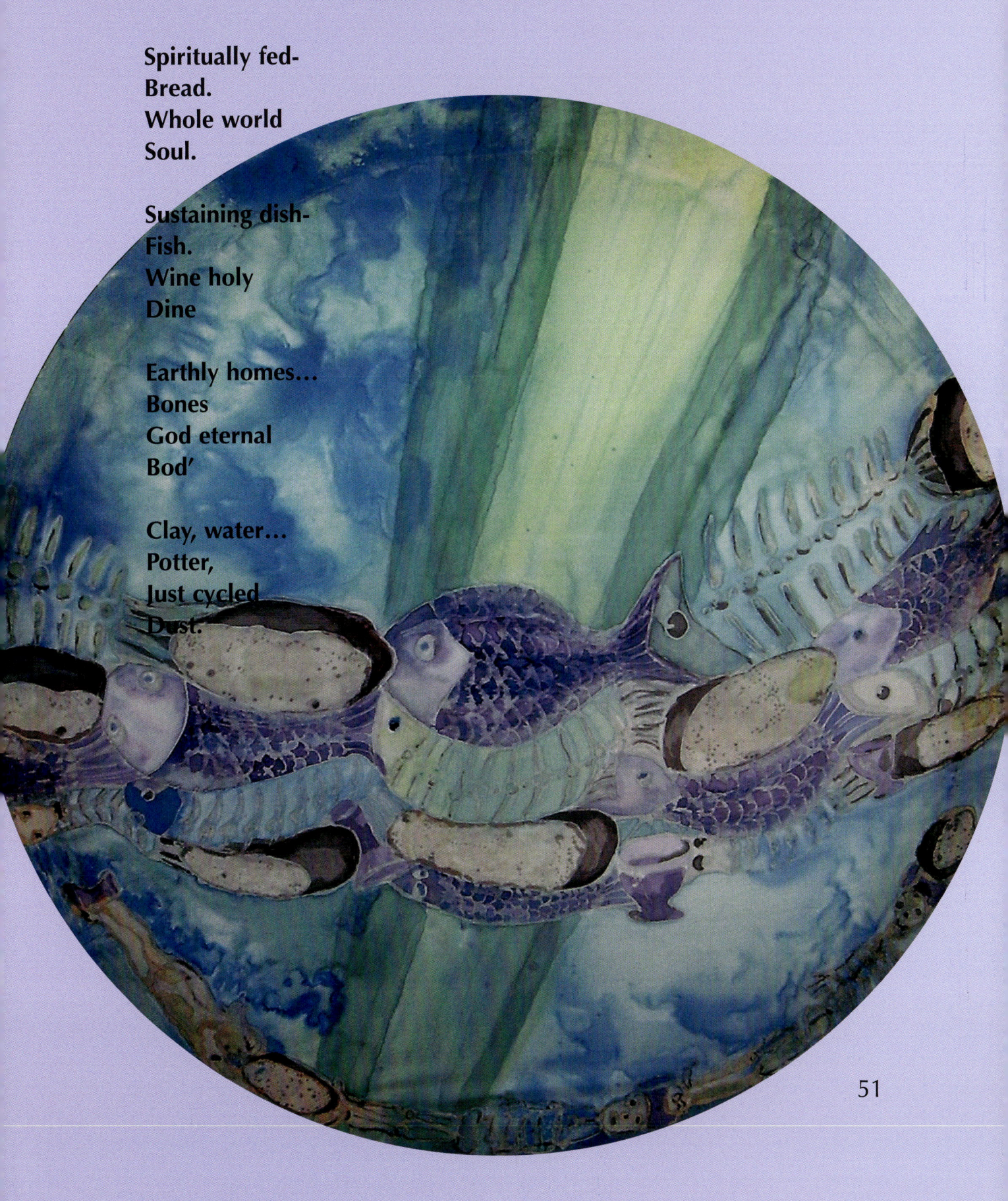

Spiritually fed-
Bread.
Whole world
Soul.

Sustaining dish-
Fish.
Wine holy
Dine

Earthly homes…
Bones
God eternal
Bod'

Clay, water…
Potter,
Just cycled
Dust.

SWEET SWEET MAPLE

Spring: season of your finest gift
Warm sun, stored in your roots
Begins to move, begins to lift
Time to don my sapping boots.

Carve the spouts of hollow sumac
Sized to fit our brace and bit.
Make tight containers, quite a knack
cut wood to feed hot fire pit.

Tap sumac into maple, gently now,
Hope sap soon begins to drip
Standing under your bare bough
Satisfying, refreshing first sweet sip.

Sit around a crackling hot fire
Watch smoking steam arise.
Meditate, tell stories, form a choir,
till sap is syrup, treasured prize.

Spring's finest gathering chore
Children shout for sweet warm spring
contained in drops, beg for more
of your sugar-life begins to sing.

Comes cold and blustery winter day
on pancakes, dried beans or bread.
Thankfully, joyfully hear us say
"Thanks to maple, we're well fed."

SWEDISH PANCAKES

For each person or two:
- Beat one egg (for pancakes use whip or electric beater)
- Add 1 Cup Milk
- Salt to taste
- 1 t. sugar
- Lightly beat in enough flour to make a very thin batter
- 1 T. butter, melted (on grill) but not hot

Beat together slightly, too much will toughen pancakes.

Preheat a large frypan (cast iron is good, and special crepe pans are available). Water drop should dance on surface. Turn to medium-high.

Ladle or use cup to drop pancake on pan, then use holder to pick pan up. Roll the pan around to distribute batter very thin. If it doesn't move out add more milk to batter in small increment. If it doesn't hold together, add more flour or egg.

Turn pancake to cook the second side, then serve.

Often eaten rolled up with maple syrup, berries, or other toppings.
Whipped cream or ice cream can make them a desert.
Cheese or meat will provide a main dish.

CONCERT IN THE SWAMP

Dusk is softly falling
Shadows lengthen
Mosquitoes calling
Tuning string section
Humming, drawling
Ummmmmmmmmmmmm

Bittern clears its throat
Guttural, throaty sound
Glunks a lower note:
Heavy rock hits water
Opening concert quote
Glunk gy younk

Soprano spring peepers
Chirp incessant lyrics
Harvest bogs:
Blueberries, cranberries,
Cattails: roots and nogs
EaTeaTeaTeaT   eaT

Minkfrog's pleasant base
Speaks of working moss
Chinking impervious face
On building logs unified
Dry babies: ancient grace
CHINKingCHINKing

Loon flies overhead…low
Journey from lake to lake
Sings crazed vibrato
As if to strike warning
Against a sneaky foe
HUEEEE mAnneN

Dry years, scary years
No available swamp hay:
Hot sun dries and sears
Silence in deadly heat
Life-death real fears

....

Where frogs and toads
once sang a concert
hot tar made into roads
Mines tear open earth
Swamps-human abodes
Rumrum Beep umrum

Can we stop destruction
halt global heating:
 indiscriminate construction
plan for wiser use
ecological instruction?
save earthsave earth save

Swamps vital to the concert
need to be protected,
tended with some effort.
Concert can continue
Vital to the world.
Greed=Greed=Greed

Sandhills squawk alarm
"learn to live with earth
or see it suffer great harm.
cut down consumption
or "lose the farm"'
beSEEEEECH teEEECH

Concert must continue
survival or our earth
depends on each of you:
world survival system
air, water and humans too
UMMMMMMMMM

SWAMP QUADRANT

Spring brings swamp to life again
Melted, warmed and budded out.
Catch the cattails brilliant green
Nogs, buttered, salted, taste superb.

In little rises find **Summer's** favorite:
Blueberries consume sun's sweetness,
Picked to make a wonderful pie or sauce.
Watery beds of wild rice: grain of life.

Frost has sweetened the cranberry,
Thickened to safe a path of ice.
Winter visit to that special bog,
Find some berries nestled in the moss?

Fall turns Cattail Nogs to ripe brown,
Brings nourishment to under water root.
Nutritious and delicious: water potato.
Also dig arrowhead: medicinal.

WAR OF OPPORTUNITY

Blessing or curse?
    Who will ever know
Will women march forward
    By becoming Army, Navy, National Guard?

Privates or generals?
    equality hard fought,
Put downs, rapes, discouragement
    Simi-official lack of encouragement.

Tradition or innovation?
    Prohibit women's equality.
Unfair acts begin making news.
    This generation pays groundbreaking dues.

Fair or foul?
    Work to prove worthy,
Suffer outrageous demands,
    when given biased commands.

Acceptance or change?
    Violence, death, ruination,
Greed leads to oppression,
    While power brings suppression.

War or Peace?
    Women choose the latter.
Meanwhile, discipline to the letter.
    Service conditions might get better.

War is not fair.

SELLING ONESELF AS A WOMAN

As I look at past generations
Many ways to sell self to accomplish needs
Have been employed:

>Molding self to please power,
>Submitting total control of decisions, actions.
>Many prostitutions.

I took a look at PERSONAL ADS
In my local underground newspaper
What would be my ad?

>"Honest, warm, monogamous, mature, honest
>enjoys organic gardening, animals, walks
>family, friends. Average appearance"

OR "Long brown hair, green eyes: arty
Funny, voluptuous, smoker, loves
Yard sales, laughing."

>Well then, let's look at MEN SEEKING WOMEN:
>"So you like dancing, motor cycles, back rubs
>And long slow kisses, 'fun'?
>Attractive? Let's hook up."

"No job, no prospects, emotionally unavailable,
big heart, gentle, self sufficient
Let me hold you all night."

>Maybe the solitary life is just fine for me.

Chapter 6

A HUNDRED YEARS OF CHANGE

BORN IN 1980
20 YEARS OLD IN 2000

Hospital, convenient for doctor, sterile, effective
Bigger town: semi-four
Less personal, mom and babe "doing well."

TIME PUSHES ME

" A woman's time now belongs to her,
she's free to decide, that's for sure."
Great, great grandmother walked three miles
To visit, then stacked hay into piles.
I line up for physical therapy at three…
Then dancing class and bowling league for me.

Great grandmother spent hours,
Sitting quietly in blueberry bowers,
While I rush hurriedly down market isles
Takes time to see fruit by the miles.
I hardly have any time for thought
So I check out to see what I've bought.

Grandmother played with her children:
Swam, adventured, read, but then was then
And now is now, I must decide. Can't say…
Amid career, travel, plays, schedule each day.
If a family would fit into my life's plan,
I would still like to be a parent if I can.

Mother studied a world of spirituality,
I don't have time to see if any of it's for me.
As for taking time to meditate,
I'm not in that desperate a state.
Women then, needed a supreme being.
I just don't have time for that type of seeing.

So women marking a path for my life
Had time to be "good" mother and wife.
Physically, mentally, spiritually strong,
Pressures on me, can't get it wrong,
So many choices, not all of them right,
I hardly have time, so busy day and night.

"In the fifties, before women 'worked'
things were just great" said a man quite irked.
' Believed they should never be given a choice,
if in their own destiny exercised any voice
it somehow diminished the life of a man?
Thanks to you, women of my past-"I Can."

PARTY LINE

Not a line of crap from a politician,
Nor a circle of friends gathering to buy certain brands*.
Not a company providing festive accouterments,
As the term might mean to us. .

No- those words meant keeping in touch
With an entire community, friends and enemies alike.
It meant no private phone calls= total access
To every one else's business.

When the box phone rang on line
Anyone and everyone could pick up on it,
As long as they were connected to "central"** by the
Same heavy black wire.

Maybe party line would be a super trade off:
For removal of spam on my computer.
Shut off unwanted messages I receive, especially
Those about viagra: real crap.

* Products marketed at "house parties" (ie Tupperware)
** Central: operator who connected one party line to outside systems

61

TECHNICALLY SPEAKING

Grandma asked me to go shopping for a cell,
saying "Things have come long way since 'ma bell'"
" Can't understand new phone language very well".

"Call waiting is standard", the sales associate said.
"Not in my book" grandma retorted and shook her head
" I don't care what any clerk says": not easily led.

"Thousands of numbers in it's memory bank"
" I don't care, just where's the phone's crank?"
our Grandma always was pretty frank."

" 'twas ours when a long two shorts would ring
No fancy sounds, music or ring a ding ding.
One or all of twenty could be rubber necking.

"Text messaging so much better than snail"
"If I want to write a letter I'll use the U.S. mail".
Our mailman will deliver, never fail."

"Another wonderful feature is our speed dial"
"I know important numbers", said grandma with a smile".
"Don't need to choose them for a special file

"You can take pictures, even record a movie".
" I used to think movies were really groovy,
but for me to phone them is really hooey."

"M3P player has countless songs you can get,
phone will connect to world- email or internet".
"Just want a phone to call out, mind's set"

Technology separates us from our past
Now things change so very fast
But values, relationships will always last.

BACK FROM IRAQ?

A long leisurely courtship would have been nice:
    He got his traveling papers from Uncle Sam,
So a hurried wedding would have to suffice.

He already was a military man when first we met,
    So I wasn't privileged to know him before
Boot camp, indoctrination hardened his mind set.

His family says he was more caring, gentle: kind
    I still love those traits but sometimes wonder
How he'd be if army hadn't changed his mind.

If he hadn't learned how to attack, kill and hate
    hadn't seen man's cruelty to man in action
If he'd never seen the countries Iraq and Kuwait.

Now he must take many pills every painful day
    Attend support groups, fight the tough image
Just to keep traumatic memories, actions away.

I wonder if nation's leaders ever know the cost
    In addition to death, loss and deprivation,
Of peace of mind, soul and body, eternally lost?

The military marriage with hopeless strain
    Was too much for over half the couples
over in less than three years- for what gain?

PURR FECT MORN…

Ragged-Rhythm tic- Rumbling
Tiger cat sings me into a new day.
Cuddled under my arm pit-
As maiden with ancient hero.

Peaceful- Contented-Hopeful
That the day will bring only good.
In step with the world of all
That's natural, joyful, purr-fect.

MAY 15, 2003

Powerful
Ethereal
Moon eclipses
Breathe crisp clean air
Clear cloudless starlight
Frogs croak throaty love songs
Coyotes yip a haunting chorus
Shimmering form defined
Glowing ball suspended
Loons discuss
Ornament
Fragile

SMOOTHIE

"You're an old smoothie"
Grandma seems to compare my favorite beverage to me.
Guess it was slang in her time for a player.
Now the word defines combination of fruits, ice, maybe milk,
all blended into a concoction which goes down smoothly.
I would never tell a guy he had really gotten to me.

"I'm an old softy"
Tough as nails, that's how I see grandma: softy...Not.
It's just an old song whose words are obsolete.
Blenders, food processors and such didn't exist back then.
How could they know great flavor combined so smoothly?
Tho I hear that they were soft in standing up to the male gender.

" Just like putty in the hands of a guy like you"
Any friend of mine respects me as an individual person,
Won't play any "romantic games", it's all out in
the open…
I will cut down on her "meat and
potato" diet, watch my figure.
For health reasons only I will
look svelte, classy, "now".
Now, what will I wear to the
stands for his football game
today?

SMOOTHY

Smoothies may be made in a blender or food processor using many combinations of fruit, milk, ice or other ingredients. Many people use them for breakfast, or pack them in an insulated container to take with them to work or recreation.

ETERNAL CIRCLE

Darkness, deep darkness
No beginning, no end
Void of form,

My living plasma alone
Existing, pulsating, moving
Only a hand

No eyes, limbs or features
No complexity, variety
Simple, alone

Past human history gone
No future of hope
Only now

No hand to rock an infant
Work, create, grow in
Empathy, joy

No gray haired wisdom
Gone camaraderie
No smiles, tears

Suddenly darkness broke
Many hands appeared
Circle of life

Past present, future
Each gender there
All ages

Let me be a part of
This great circle
Infinity

And I awoke